I Have a Dream

THE STORY OF MARTIN LUTHER KING

I Have a Dream

BY MARGARET DAVIDSON

Scholastic Inc.

New York   Toronto   London   Auckland   Sydney

For Ed Fisher

Grateful acknowledgement is made to Joan Daves and the Estate of Martin Luther King, Jr., for the use of copyrighted material from Dr. King's speeches and commentary. Copyright © 1955, 1956, 1963, 1965, 1968 by Martin Luther King, Jr. and the Estate of Martin Luther King, Jr. Reprinted by permission of Joan Daves.

On the cover: *Martin Luther King and his daughter Yolanda, 1964 Photo © 1985 Flip Schulke/Black Star.*

Reading level is determined by using the Spache Readability Formula. 3.0 signifies low 3rd-grade level.

ISBN 0-590-41291-4

Copyright © 1986 by Margaret Davidson

12 11 10 9 8 7 6 5 4 3   8 9/8 0 1/9

"You Are as Good as Anyone."

It was a fine fall day in Atlanta, Georgia— a perfect day to do things outside. Martin had just come home from school. Quickly he changed his good school clothes. Then he ran across the street to the house where his two best friends lived. They were brothers. And for as long as Martin could remember the three of them had played together.

Now, as he had done so many times before, six-year-old Martin knocked on their front door. His friends' mother opened it.

But she didn't smile, or even say hello.

Finally Martin broke the strange silence. "Can Tom and Billy come out and play?"

"No," she answered, "they can't."

Martin was puzzled. This was what she'd said yesterday, too. "Are they sick?" he asked.

"No," she answered, "they're not sick. Just run along now, Martin."

But Martin kept on. "Can they play tomorrow?"

The woman sighed. "Now, look here, Martin." Her voice was not angry. But it was very, very firm. "It was all right for you to play together when you were younger. But now you're all in school. So it's best that you go your own different ways."

Not be best friends anymore? "Why?" Martin whispered.

"Because you're colored and we're white," the boys' mother answered. Then she shut the door.

Colored? White? Martin held out his hands. Yes, they were colored. They were colored a kind of medium brown. But that was just a fact—a fact like the sky was blue and the grass was green. What did it have to do with friendship?

Martin felt heavy and hurt and all mixed up. He decided to ask his mother what this was all about.

Martin's mother took him on her lap. She wiped away the tears from his cheeks. Then she began to talk. She told Martin about a time long ago when men and women and children as young as he was had been taken from their homes in Africa. She talked about how they had been brought here to America and sold as slaves.

She looked at him. "Do you know what a slave is?" she asked. Martin shook his head.

"Being a slave means being owned by someone. Owned the way we own a dog or a car or a washing machine. It means being somebody else's property and having to do whatever they want you to do. It means not having any freedom at all."

Martin's mother paused for a moment and then she went on. "Here in the South millions of slaves worked in white people's homes and businesses and farms. Then a war broke out between the northern and southern states. The North won the Civil War—and the slaves were all freed."

Martin's eyes began to shine. Free! Maybe this wasn't such a bad story, after all.

"Yes, the Negroes were free," his mother continued. "But our troubles weren't over. Even now, in the 1930's, we still have to live with prejudice."

"Pre-ju . . . ?" It was plain that Martin didn't understand the word.

"Prejudice means that many white people cannot accept black folks as equals. They don't think we're as good as they are."

Black folks? Once more Martin held out

his hands. "But I'm brown," he said, "not black."

His mother smiled a little. "I know, Martin. Black is just another word for Negro." But her smile faded as she went on with the story. As Martin said years later, it was a story every black mother had to tell her children, sooner or later.

"Because they wanted to keep Negroes in their place, they started practicing something called segregation."

Once more Martin was puzzled. "Maybe you've had enough big words for today," his mother said. "Why don't you run out and play?"

But Martin begged her to go on. He was never satisfied with words or ideas he didn't understand. His mother sighed and said, "Well, segregation means separate, Martin. Negroes have to live completely separate lives from white people. Separate in almost every way. That's what your friends' mother was taking about."

Martin nodded. He was beginning to

understand. Suddenly he thought about the signs. He was only six and just beginning school. But he could already read. Lately he'd been reading more and more signs. Signs that said things like "No Negroes Allowed" and "Whites Only."

Then he thought about the section of Atlanta where he lived. Almost no white families lived there. He thought about the school he went to. There were no white children in it at all.

Now his mother set him on his feet. "That's enough for today," she said firmly. "So scoot."

But as Martin turned to go she held him back for a moment. "I've given you a great deal to think about today, son. Much of it you'll probably forget. But there's one thing I do want you to remember. You must never feel that you are less than other people. You are as good as anyone."

"I'm Going to Get Me Some Big Words. . . ."

You are as good as anyone. Martin Luther King, Jr., never forgot those words. How could he—when he saw his own father bring them to life so often?

Daddy King, as most people called him, was a fighter. The first thing he fought was poverty. He was a sharecropper's son. His family never owned anything at all. The tumbledown shack they lived in, the land they farmed, even the mule that pulled the plow—everything belonged to a white farmer down the road.

Martin (on the right) was 10 years old when he posed with his older sister and younger brother in this family portrait. He was born on January 15, 1929.

Martin loved to hear his father talk about the mule. "Every morning I had to brush that animal," Daddy King remembered. "Well, I'm here to tell you that mules smell. Of course that smell just naturally rubbed off on me. So my friends began to tease me about that old mule smell. They were only joking, but finally I got mad. 'I may *smell* like a mule,' I told them one day, 'but I don't *think* like a mule!'"

No, Daddy King was smart. He knew he had to leave the land that would never belong to his family. When he was only fifteen he went to Atlanta. For many years he worked hard by day and studied hard by night. It was slow going. But now he was the Reverend Martin Luther King, Sr.—head of Ebenezer Baptist Church. Ebenezer was one of the biggest black churches in the city of Atlanta, Georgia.

Daddy King fought for an education. He fought for a good life for himself and for his family. He also fought for what he thought was right. And he wasn't afraid of anyone.

One day he and Martin were driving around in the family car. A white policeman signaled for him to pull over. "Show me your license, boy," the policeman said. This was the way white people often spoke to Negro men. It was another way they had of keeping black people in their place.

Daddy King looked at him hard. Then he pointed to Martin. "Do you see this child here?" he said in a quiet but very firm voice. "That is a *boy*. I am a *man*."

Not long after, he and Martin took a walk and happened to pass a big shoe store. Martin needed shoes, so they went inside and sat down in some seats near the door.

Suddenly a clerk was standing in front of them. "What do you think you're doing? You know you can't sit here," he said.

"There's nothing wrong with these seats," Daddy King answered. "They're quite comfortable, in fact."

The clerk's face grew red. "You know that Negroes have to sit in the back of the store. That's the rule. So you might as well stop being high and mighty and take it like the rest!"

Now Daddy King got angry. "We'll buy shoes sitting here, or we won't buy shoes at all!" Then he grabbed Martin's hand and stamped out of the store.

His anger frightened Martin a little. Finally he tugged on his father's hand. "I don't understand," he said in a small voice. "The front and the back of the store looked the same to me."

Daddy King took a couple of deep breaths. "It's just another example of segregation, Martin," he said more calmly. "Just another way of keeping us down." Then suddenly his voice rose in anger again. "I will never accept this stupid, cruel system," he said. "I'll fight it until the day I die!"

Martin looked up at his father. "If you are against it, so am I," he said. At that moment he was very glad that he'd been named after his father.

As a minister's son Martin spent many hours each week in church. "Ebenezer was like a second home to me," he always said. How he loved to hear his father preach. The Reverend King's deep voice filled the church like organ music. And the words he spoke made Martin very proud. They sounded so fine and fancy. "You just wait," he whispered to his mother one day. "I'm going to get *me* some big words, too."

And he did. Learning was always easy for Martin. "I like to get in over my head, and then puzzle things out," he said. No wonder he was usually at the head of his class. Except for one subject, that is— spelling. He was never a very good speller. "I was horrible at it then, and I'm horrible at it now," he admitted—even after he was grown and had written several books.

Martin's two closest playmates were his older sister Chris, and his little brother A.D. But he had many other friends. Most of them called him M.L.

He and his friends roller-skated down the rough sidewalks in front of their homes, and swooped through the streets on their bikes. They made model airplanes and flew kites high in the sky.

They played baseball or football in an empty field behind the King house. Martin was small for his age, but he was tough. "He just wouldn't quit," a friend said. "He ran right over anybody who got in the way." So he was always one of the first to be picked for any team.

Martin was tough, but he didn't like to get into fights. "It makes me feel bad inside," he explained. So he found another way to handle trouble. He talked his way out of it.

One of his playmates spoke about his way with words. "That M.L.—even when he was just a bitty boy, he could talk you into or out of *anything.*"

A Dream Begins to Grow

Martin had some grand times with his friends. But sometimes he said, "No, not now," when they came to play. For he also needed time to think and daydream and read.

Books were a kind of magic for Martin. They took him so many places. They told him so many new things. Most important, they introduced him to so many people who became heroes in his life. For Martin's favorite books were about black history, and the men and women who had made it.

He read about Harriet Tubman, the slave who escaped to freedom in the North before the Civil War, and yet returned South again and again to lead other slaves to freedom.

He read about Frederick Douglass, another slave who escaped to freedom but never forgot his people. Douglass was a great speaker. For years he traveled around the northern states and England telling audiences about what it felt like to be a slave. And after the Civil War he continued to work for basic human rights for all.

Martin read about the great teacher Booker T. Washington, who in the late 1800's founded Tuskegee Institute in Alabama—the first college for black people.

He read about George Washington Carver, the scientist who worked at Tuskegee and found ways to make many useful products out of such plants as sweet potatoes and soybeans and peanuts.

And he read about people who were doing exciting things right that minute. He read about the singer and actor Paul

Robeson, who became famous around the world. He read about people like the boxer Joe Louis—the Brown Bomber, as many people were calling him—who in 1937 became heavyweight champion of the world. And the track star Jesse Owens, who won four gold medals for the United States in the 1936 Olympic games.

As Martin read about these men and women who had done such big things, a dream began to grow inside him. He wanted to do something big, something important with his life, too.

But what? Martin wasn't sure. Not yet. But he did know one thing. Whatever he grew up to be, he wanted to help his people. He wanted to make their lives better.

Once Martin's mother had said that segregation meant separate. But Martin was old enough now to know it meant

Among the black men Martin admired were track star Jesse Owens, educator Booker T. Washington, scientist George Washington Carver, and singer Paul Robeson (dressed here in his costume for the opera Othello).

more than that. It meant unequal, too. For in almost every way a Negro's life was made less by it.

Martin had plenty to eat and wear. His family owned a nice house. His father was a respected minister. But Martin knew that most others were not so lucky.

Usually, black children went to the worst schools. They lived in the most run-down houses. When they grew up they had to take the hard jobs, the dirty jobs that no one else wanted. And they were paid far less money than whites, too.

Martin was protected from some of the worst effects of segregation. But it touched his life all the same. He was in high school when his English teacher picked him to represent the school in a statewide speech contest.

On the day of the contest he and the teacher, Miss Sarah Bradley, traveled several hundred miles by bus to the town of Valdosta. There Martin gave his speech and won second prize in the whole state.

After the contest he and Miss Bradley got back on the bus and headed for home. They sat toward the back, for that was the law. Blacks sat in the back of any bus, and whites sat in the front.

Martin and his teacher had a lot to talk about—his speech and all the others that had been given. They didn't notice when the bus stopped to pick up more passengers. They didn't notice when all the seats filled up and some white people had to stand in the aisle. But the bus driver did. He stopped the bus and came back to where Martin and Miss Bradley were sitting. "Come on, get up," he said gruffly. "Give those seats over."

Martin stared up at him. *Why should I?* he thought. *I paid for this seat. And I was here first.*

The bus driver saw that Martin wasn't planning to move. And he turned ugly. "Listen, you," he snarled. "You get out of that seat or I call the cops!"

Martin felt Miss Bradley pluck at his

sleeve. "Come on, Martin," she said quietly. "I don't want you to get hurt. Besides, it's the law."

"It's a bad law!" Martin snapped.

He didn't mind bringing trouble on himself, but he didn't want to bring it on Miss Bradley. So finally he stood up. He stood for ninety long and bitter miles before the bus finally pulled into Atlanta. "That night will never leave my mind," Martin Luther King was to say many times later. "It was the angriest I have ever been in my life."

Martin was such a good student that he skipped several grades in school. So he was only 15 when he entered Atlanta's Morehouse College. Most of the students entering college were 18 or 19.

Martin loved college life. Morehouse was a tough school and he had to work hard. But as usual he found time to enjoy himself as well. He belonged to a number of clubs. His favorite was the glee club, where he could let his rich baritone voice soar. He tried out for the football team. And he never had any trouble getting a date. "That Martin," his brother A.D. said later. "He sure had a way with girls. They just loved all that smooth talk of his. And he was the best dancer in town."

One of the clubs Martin joined was a discussion club—a place to talk about your ideas and listen to the ideas of others. Morehouse was a black college, but white students from other nearby colleges belonged to the club, too.

For the first time since he'd been a boy of six, Martin got to know some white people as friends. He admitted later that he had come close to turning his back on the whole white race. "But as I got to see more of white people in this club," he said, "my anger softened. I began to see that they weren't the enemy. The evil was segregation itself."

Martin began to think more and more about his future. He knew he wanted to make a difference in people's lives. But how? *Maybe I'll become a doctor,* he thought at first. *That would be a good way to help poor people.*

Next he thought he might be a lawyer. Then he could fight for his people's rights in the courts.

There was one thing he did *not* want to become—a minister.

Of course his father was a minister and Martin respected his father. And he always felt a sense of coming home whenever he was in church. But many other black ministers in the South had no education. All they had was emotion. So they shouted and yelled and stamped their feet instead of using their minds. Martin worshipped words and the ideas behind words, so this sort of thing made him very uncomfortable. He didn't want to be like them.

But then Martin thought of his teachers at Morehouse. Many of them were ministers, too. *They* were educated. *They* talked about interesting and important things. Maybe being a minister wasn't so bad. . . .

One of these men was Dr. Benjamin Mays, President of Morehouse. He watched this bright student who was struggling so hard trying to decide what his life work would be. "Look, Martin," he finally said. "There's nothing wrong with emotion—if it goes hand in hand with solid thinking. Besides, you say you want to help your people. Where can you help them more? The church is the heart of our community. It's where you can reach the most people at one time."

Martin knew this was true. *Is this what I'm meant to be?* he asked himself now. And the answer came back loud and clear— *yes.*

Daddy King was pleased with Martin's decision. But he wanted Martin to be sure he had a true calling. "Are you sure you can stir people, M.L.?" he asked. "Are you sure you really have a gift?"

"I'll show you by preaching a sermon," 17-year-old Martin answered.

Martin was going to deliver that sermon in one of the smaller meeting rooms at Ebenezer. But word had got around the church that Daddy King's son was going to preach his first sermon.

More and more people poured into the little room. Soon it was packed to over-flowing. Finally everyone had to move to the main part of the church.

Martin stood behind the pulpit, looking down at all those faces. Many of those people had known him all his life. For a moment he felt nervous. Then he took a deep breath and began to speak. And the words he had always loved did not fail him.

He spoke about his vision of God. "God isn't just some distant figure, high on a throne in the sky," he said. "God is *here*. God is *now*. God is in each and every one of you. And because God is inside you, you have *value*. You *matter*."

"Amen!" someone said.

"You tell them, M.L.!" another person exclaimed.

Daddy King began to smile. No doubt about it—his boy had the gift.

Some Big Ideas

Martin graduated from Morehouse College when he was 19 years old. He was still very young. But Daddy King thought he was old enough to become an assistant pastor at Ebenezer. Martin didn't agree. He felt he needed more education to become the kind of minister he wanted to be. So in the fall of 1948 he enrolled at Crozer Theological Seminary in Chester, Pennsylvania.

Crozer brought real changes to Martin's life. For the first time he was away from home. Away from all the people who loved him. And for the first time he was living in an integrated world. There were only six black students at Crozer—the other one hundred were white.

At first this made Martin nervous. He felt he had to be extra careful, extra neat, extra polite. But most of the students seemed eager to be friends. They seemed to be saying, Hey, we're interested in *you*, not the color of your skin. So soon Martin began to relax and become his natural outgoing self again.

He had some wonderful times with these new friends. But as usual he also took his studies seriously. Once he had said to his mother, "I'm going to get me some big words!" Now, at Crozer, he set out to get some big ideas. Some ideas to help him lead a truly good life.

He read the words of the man he was named for. Martin Luther was a sixteenth century religious leader who had brought about many changes in the church. He said, "To go against your conscience—your sense of right and wrong—is neither safe nor right."

Then there was another religious leader, Reinhold Niebuhr, who wrote, "Men in groups commit greater crimes and sins than they do as individuals."

Of course he studied the words of Jesus—"Love your enemies," and "He who lives by the sword shall die by the sword."

And one of his childhood heroes, Frederick Douglass—"If there is no struggle, there is no progress."

He was also impressed by a writer and philosopher who lived in New England a hundred years before. Henry David Thoreau believed that "If a law is unjust, men should refuse to cooperate with it. They should even be willing to go to jail for not obeying such a law." Thoreau called this civil disobedience.

Civil disobedience. The first time Martin read those words he whispered them aloud. He certainly did like the sound of them.

Then one day Martin heard a lecture by a teacher who had just come back from India. The people there had been ruled by England for many, many years. But in 1947 they were able to form a government of their own—because of a man named Mahatma Gandhi.

Gandhi had led this successful revolution of his people without firing a shot. For he, too, like Thoreau, believed in not obeying unjust laws. And being willing to go to jail. But he also believed in one more thing. Gandhi believed that no matter what you did to protest wrong—whether it was a strike or a boycott or a march or a demonstration—you must never use violence.

He called this *nonviolent resistance,* or *love-force.* "I want to touch your hearts," Gandhi said to his enemies. "Only then will you change."

Nonviolence . . . a revolution based on love, not hate. . . . These ideas stirred Mar-

Long after he left college, Martin continued to be inspired by India's nonviolent leader, Mahatma Gandhi.

tin deeply. But he had no idea that one day a revolution based on love and nonviolent resistance would change his life—and the lives of millions of others as well.

Right now Martin was busy becoming Crozer's top student. "We have just finished a period of examinations," one of his teachers wrote, "and the only man who was granted honors in them was King. . . . He seems to know where he wants to go and how to get there."

In the spring of 1951 Martin graduated from Crozer with a straight "A" average. Not only that, he was named the Seminary's most outstanding student. And he also won a prize of $1,200. He decided to use this money to work toward the highest degree in education—a doctorate—at Boston University in Massachusetts.

That was a very happy time for Martin. Only one thing seemed missing. As usual he dated a lot of different girls. But none of them really captured his heart.

Then one day a friend introduced him to a young music student who was also studying in Boston. Her name was Coretta Scott.

Martin and Coretta found they had much in common. They were both from the South. They both loved music, books, and talking about ideas. Before the end of their first date Martin announced, "You have everything I ever wanted in a wife. There are only four things, and you have them all."

Coretta was stunned. "I don't see how you can say that," she said. "You don't even know me."

"Yes," Martin answered with complete certainty. "I can tell. The four things that I am looking for in a wife are character, intelligence, personality, and beauty. And you have them all."

Soon Martin did ask Coretta to marry him. She didn't say yes—not right away. She loved him. She knew that already. But she had a dream, too. She wanted to be a professional singer. Also, she did not want to marry a minister and become a minister's wife. It sounded so dull to her.

One day she wrote about her worries in a letter to her sister Edythe. Her sister had met Martin, and wrote back, "Don't have silly doubts, Coretta. If you love him, go ahead and marry him. You won't have the career you dreamed of, but you'll have a career. You will not be marrying any ordinary minister."

Martin and Coretta are married by his father, Daddy King, on June 18, 1953.

The Man and the Movement Meet

On a warm June day in 1953 Martin and Coretta were married. During the next year they finished their studies in Boston. Now Martin was Dr. Martin Luther King, Jr. It was time to make a big decision. What next?

Martin had been offered a number of different jobs. Three churches wanted him to preach. Three colleges asked him to come and teach. The world of ideas would always attract Martin. "I'd love to be a teacher someday," he told Coretta. "But for now I want to be a pastor."

Where, though? Two of the churches that offered him a job were in the North. The third was in the deep South. Did they want to go south again—south to where segregation was still a way of life?

Still, the South was their home, and they loved it in spite of everything. Besides, Martin felt that something was stirring in the South. The United States Supreme Court had just ruled that separate schools for blacks and whites were unconstitutional—they were against the law of the land. The Court was saying what Martin had known all his life—separate *is* unequal.

Martin thought of segregation as a wall—a wall separating the lives of blacks and whites. This Supreme Court ruling was the first break in that wall. Martin wanted to be there to help take down more of it. So he acepted the offer of the

Dexter Avenue Baptist Church in Montgomery, Alabama.

Now it was the morning of December 2, 1955. Martin and Coretta had been in Montgomery for a little over a year—a happy year of settling into a new marriage and a new life. And they had just become parents. They named the baby Yolanda. But from the first they called her Yoki. She was now just two weeks old.

Martin was sitting in his study working on next Sunday's sermon when the phone rang. As he reached for it he could hear Coretta in the kitchen. She was singing softly while she finished the breakfast dishes. He could hear Yoki fussing a little in the back bedroom. Everything was so normal. There was nothing to tell him that this telephone call would change his life forever.

It was Ed Nixon, one of Montgomery's black leaders. "Martin," he said, "they just arrested another of our people for not standing up. I say we should do something about it this time."

Martin knew exactly what Ed Nixon was talking about. Montgomery was one of the most segregated cities in America. The two races did almost nothing together. There was even a city law that said blacks and whites could not play cards or checkers with each other. And one of the worst parts of this segregated life-style was the Montgomery bus system.

Negroes sat in the back of the bus and whites sat in the front. The first four rows of any bus were for white passengers only. Even if these seats were empty, no black could sit in them. If a bus was full and more whites got on, blacks had to give up their seats and stand.

But on Thursday, December 1, 1955, a woman named Rosa Parks refused. She had worked hard all day at her job in a downtown department store. After work she'd done some shopping. Now she was finally on her way home. Sighing with relief, she sank into one of the seats right behind the "Whites Only" section.

A few blocks later the bus stopped and more passengers got on, most of them white. But all the seats were taken. "Get up," the bus driver said to the black passengers sitting around Rosa Parks.

Everyone obeyed—except Rosa Parks. She just sat there. The driver told her to get up again. And still she sat. "Look, I'm going to have to call the cops if you don't get up," the driver threatened. But even this didn't work. So Rosa Parks was arrested and fined fourteen dollars for breaking one of Montgomery's segregation laws.

"I don't know why I wouldn't move," Mrs. Parks said later. "There was no plan at all. I was just tired. My feet hurt."

But Martin Luther King had another explanation. He said that Rosa Parks had been tracked down by the Zeitgeist—the spirit of the times. What he didn't realize was that the Zeitgeist had tracked him down, too. The civil rights movement was about to begin.

Rosa Parks speaks to a reporter after her arrest. She was arrested because she refused to give her seat to a white person on a crowded bus.

That evening Martin and a number of other black leaders gathered together at Martin's church. They decided to call for a boycott on Monday, December 5. On that day they wanted all black riders to stay off the buses.

But how could they get this message to

the 50,000 Negroes who lived in so many different parts of town? Church women volunteered to print and hand out leaflets which said:

"Don't ride the bus to work, to town, to school, or any place Monday, December 5. Another Negro woman has been arrested because she refused to give up her bus seat. Come to a mass meeting, Monday at seven at the Holt Street Baptist Church for further instructions."

The ministers also agreed to talk about the boycott in their Sunday sermons. But all weekend Martin and Coretta worried. They knew that many Negroes were afraid to do anything that might anger white people. Others might simply not care enough to take a stand.

"I think we should be happy if half of the riders stay off the buses," Martin said to Coretta on Sunday evening. "Any more than that will be a truly great victory."

Martin and Coretta were up before dawn the next day. The first bus of the day was due to pass their house at six. Coretta stood at the living room window, peering out into the gloom. Martin was in the kitchen, pouring a cup of coffee.

Suddenly, "Martin, Martin, come quickly!" she called. He got to her side just as a completely empty bus rolled past—a bus that was usually packed with blacks going to work. Fifteen minutes later the next bus appeared. It, too, was empty. There were two people on the third bus— both of them white.

Martin and Coretta hugged each other. "Corrie, it's a miracle!" Martin Luther King kept saying. "A miracle is happening in this town today!"

And so it was. All day long people walked—some as many as fourteen miles. And the buses stayed empty. Someone saw a very old woman hobbling down the street. "Why didn't you stay home today, Granny?" he asked her. "It wouldn't have made much difference."

"I'm not walking for myself," she answered. "I'm walking for my children and grandchildren."

Late that afternoon Martin and the other leaders gathered together once more. The one-day boycott was a complete success. Should they be satisfied with that? Or should they continue it until something really changed? The answer came quickly—continue!

At the meeting they formed an organization to direct the boycott. It was called the Montgomery Improvement Association—MIA for short. But who would lead it?

They needed someone who could talk to *all* the black people of Montgomery—educated and ignorant alike. Martin had only been in Montgomery for a year. But already he was known as "the friendly pastor" because he treated everyone the same way.

"I nominate the Reverend King," a voice called out. A vote was taken, and everyone agreed. Martin would be their new leader.

As soon as he got home he told Coretta what had happened. His days were already very busy. This would mean much more time spent away from her and the baby. "And I must be truthful," he said. "This could become dangerous."

But Coretta didn't hesitate. "Martin, you know that whatever you do, you have my backing," she said.

Martin's first duty as president of the MIA was to give a speech at the mass meeting that night. So now he went into his study and closed the door. He looked at the clock. It said six-thirty—and the meeting was due to start at seven. It often took him fifteen or twenty hours to prepare a single Sunday sermon. Now he had fifteen or twenty minutes to prepare what he somehow knew was going to be the most important speech of his life.

In those few minutes, he had to work out a way to stir the people to action and

yet quiet the anger they must be feeling. Anger that could so easily lead to violence.

All too soon it was time to go. Martin was still five blocks away from the church when he realized something amazing was going on. Cars were jamming the road. The sidewalks were filled with people. *They're all going to the meeting!* he thought.

The leaders had expected four or five hundred. But at least a thousand people packed the church that evening. Four thousand more stood outside, waiting to hear his speech. Loudspeakers were quickly set up for these people.

The meeting began with all five thousand singing, "Onward, Christian Soldiers." Martin said later, "The roar of their voices was like an echo of Heaven itself."

Then it was time for him to speak. And from somewhere deep inside himself he found just the right words. First he told the story of Rosa Parks. Then he spoke

Martin accepts the presidency of the newly-formed Montgomery Improvement Association.

about the treatment all Negroes so often got on the buses.

"But there comes a time when people get tired," he said. "We are here this evening to say to those who have mistreated us so long that we are *tired—tired* of being segregated and humiliated; *tired* of being kicked about. . . ."

His deep voice rolled out powerfully as he spoke about self-respect. "For many years we have shown amazing patience. We have sometimes given our white brothers the feeling that we liked the way we were being treated. But we come here tonight to be saved—saved from patience that makes us patient with *anything* less than freedom and justice."

People started to stamp their feet and cheer. "Tell it to them, Doc!" one voice called. "Amen!" another shouted.

Martin waited until they grew quiet again and then he spoke about love and nonviolence. "Once again we must hear the words of Jesus echoing across the centuries: 'Love your enemies, bless them that curse you, and pray for them that despitefully use you.' In spite of the mistreatment that we have confronted, we must not become bitter, and end up hating our white brothers. As Booker T. Washington said, 'Let no man pull you so low as to make you hate him.'"

And finally, "If we protest courageously, and yet with dignity and Christian love, when the history books are written in the future, somebody will have to say, 'There lived a race of people—of black people—who had the moral courage to stand up for their rights. And thereby they injected a new meaning into the veins of history and civilization.'"

For a moment there was silence. Then all across the church, and in the street outside, people clapped and shouted and cheered and wept for joy.

One of the men who had voted for Martin that afternoon summed up what everyone was feeling. "My God," he said, "I thought we were just electing an agreeable guy. Instead we got Moses!"

Moses—the Old Testament prophet who led his people out of slavery and into the Promised Land.

The Walking City

In the beginning the Montgomery Improvement Association asked for only three things. They wanted seating on a first-come, first-serve basis. This meant putting an end to the hated "Whites Only" section. They wanted drivers to treat black passengers politely. And they wanted some black drivers hired to drive buses in mainly black parts of town.

But the city and the bus company would not agree even to these simple demands. So the boycott continued. One of the first things the MIA did was organize a car-pool—a group of drivers willing to take people where they needed to go. Almost overnight 300 people volunteered their cars and time. But still many, many people had to walk.

Martin was amazed by their spirit. "Now listen," he said one day to an old woman called Mother Pollard, "you've been with us from the beginning. But you're too old to keep walking, so I want you to start riding the bus again."

"Oh, no," she said. "I'm gonna walk just as long as everybody else walks. I'm gonna walk till it's over."

"But aren't your feet tired?" Martin asked.

"Yes," she answered. "My feet is tired, but my soul is at rest."

City officials didn't understand this spirit. At first they treated the boycott like some kind of a joke. After all, it was December now and the weather was gray and chill. "Just you wait until the first day it rains," they said. "That will get them back on the buses." The next day it rained, and the people still walked.

So little by little it began to sink in—these people were serious. The city began to fight back. First they tried trickery. They simply announced that the MIA had called the boycott off. It was all right to go back on the buses. They planned to run this story on page one of the city's biggest newspaper.

Luckily Martin and the other MIA leaders heard about this fake story. But how could they get word to their people before the newspaper appeared?

It happened to be Saturday night—an evening many people spent out having a good time. So Martin and his aides, the people who worked most closely with him, got in their cars and visited as many restaurants, social clubs, dance halls, and bars as they could. It was almost dawn before Martin got home—dog-tired. But the long night's effort had been worth it. The buses remained empty.

Next the city officials tried to turn the

people against Martin. By now the boycott was national news. Contributions to keep it going were coming in from all over the country. So the city said that Martin Luther King was putting much of this money into his own pocket. He was getting rich off the movement.

This false rumor really hurt Martin. What if even some of the people believed it? It could be the end of the movement. "I almost broke down under it," he said. Finally, at one of the mass meetings that the MIA held every week, he offered to resign.

All around the church people were suddenly on their feet. "No! No!" they shouted. "You're our man!"

So trickery hadn't worked. Neither had false rumors. Now the city turned tough. The mayor went on television and warned that from now on they were going to "stop pussyfooting around with this boycott."

Next day the police began arresting car-pool drivers for any reason they could think of. Before long Martin was arrested, too—for going thirty in a twenty-five-mile-an-hour zone. He was taken to the city jail and thrown in a filthy, smelly cell with drunks and thieves and murderers.

Martin felt stunned by what he saw and felt. All his life he'd been told only bad people went to jail. Now, as he said, "Strange gusts of emotion swept through me like cold winds." He could not know how many times he would have to go to jail in the years to come.

He didn't stay there long this time. News of his arrest spread quickly, and people began to gather at the jail. Soon a huge crowd was milling around in front of it. When the jailer saw how angry they were, he panicked. He personally escorted this troublemaking preacher out of the building.

That evening at still another mass meeting Martin spoke about his experience. "If we are arrested every day, if we are exploited every day, if we are tram-

Martin is arrested for the first time.

pled over every day, don't ever let anyone pull you so low as to hate them. We must realize so many people are taught to hate us that they are not totally responsible for their hate."

But hate *was* getting him down. Every day thirty to forty ugly letters arrived at his home. They contained messages like, "If you think you are as good as white people you are sadly mistaken," and, "Get out of town before it's too late."

The letters were bad. The telephone

calls were worse. All day and into the night the phone would ring. Often when Martin or Coretta picked it up they simply heard the sound of someone spitting into the receiver. Other times callers spewed out long strings of curse words. Still others threatened to kill not only Martin, but Coretta and baby Yoki, too.

Often he looked at his wife and tiny child—the daughter he called "the darling of my life"—and thought, *Some people out there want them to die. They can be taken away from me at any moment. Or I can be taken from them.*

Later Martin told a friend how he felt then. "I was so tired. And cold fingers of fear were creeping up my soul."

Late one night the phone rang. Martin snatched it up before it could wake Coretta. He wasn't surprised when an ugly voice whispered in his ear, "If you aren't out of this town in three days we gonna blow your brains out."

Martin slipped out of bed and went to the kitchen. *I can't take it anymore,* he thought as he poured himself a cup of coffee. *I'll have to quit. There is no other choice.* He had never felt so alone.

Now he began to pray out loud. "Lord, I'm down here trying to do what is right. But Lord, I must confess that I'm weak. I'm afraid. The people are looking to me for leadership. If I stand before them without strength or courage, they, too, will falter. I am at the end of my powers. I have nothing left. I can't face it alone."

Then suddenly, at this lowest moment of his life, he seemed to hear a voice. A voice so clear that it seemed to come from everywhere. "Martin Luther," the voice said, "stand up for right. Stand up for justice. Stand up for truth. And I will be with you, even unto the end of the world."

Suddenly Martin was filled with an inner calm and strength he had never felt before. *I can face anything,* he thought. *I can stand up without fear.* All because of a voice that had promised "never to leave me, never to leave me alone."

The Miracle of Montgomery

Martin needed that new strength very soon. Three nights later, while he was at a meeting, he received some terrible news. His house had been bombed. The whole front had been blown away. Martin raced home, thinking of only one thing. Coretta! Yoki! Were they all right?

Luckily they were. Coretta had been in the living room when she heard a thud on the front porch. She thought someone had thrown a brick—it had happened before. But she decided to go to the back of the house anyway. When the bomb exploded she was safe.

Now Martin hugged her hard. Then he felt a hand on his arm. It was one of his aides. "Doc, you've got to come out and talk to them," the man said. "They're getting out of hand."

A large crowd of Negroes had gathered outside. They were angry about the bombing. They were ready to go after any white people in sight. As Martin held up his hands to get their attention he heard one man shout at a white policeman, "I've got my gun and you've got yours. So let's shoot it out!"

Quickly Martin began to speak. "My wife and baby are all right. So don't panic. Don't do anything panicky at all. Don't get your weapons.

"We are not advocating violence," Martin continued. "I want you to love your enemies. Love them and let them know you love them. I want it to be known the length and breadth of the land that if

I am stopped, the movement will not stop. If I am stopped our work will not stop, for what we are doing is right.

"Remember the words of Jesus, 'He who lives by the sword shall perish by the sword.' We must meet our white brothers' hate with love."

The crowd stared at him. How could a man whose house had just been bombed— a man whose wife and child had barely escaped being killed—how could he say such things?

At last one old man broke the silence. "God bless you, son," he said. "Amen to that," others added, as they began to drift away.

I want it to be known the length and breadth of the land, he had said. And it was. More and more reporters had been coming to Montgomery in the last few weeks. Now the story of this young black preacher who stood in front of his bombed house and talked about love and nonviolence became news all over the country.

But still the city of Montgomery refused to give in. Next they took Martin to court. They said the movement was breaking an old antiboycott law. It was interfering with a lawful business—the bus company—without "just cause."

Lawyers for the MIA built a strong case to show that blacks did have "just cause" to boycott the buses. But Martin had little hope they would win the case—not before a white judge. He was right. The judge found Martin guilty.

Martin's lawyers said they would take the case to a higher court. A huge crowd was waiting outside. As soon as they caught sight of Martin coming out of the courthouse they broke into cheers.

"Hail King!" a man cried.

"Hail the King!" someone else shouted.

"King *is* King!" another yelled.

"What happens now, Dr. King?" a reporter called out.

Martin smiled as he looked at the proud and happy people. "The movement goes on!" he answered.

Later that reporter talked to a friend. "You know," he said, "I've seen many mass movements, but nothing like this. It is one of laughter and song."

Now the Montgomery Improvement Association went to court. They asked a federal court to end all bus segregation in Montgomery. They said that it was unconstitutional—it was against the Constitution of the United States.

In May of 1956 the federal judges ruled in favor of the MIA. It was a big victory for the movement. But the city *still* refused to give up. They said they would take the case to the Supreme Court—the highest court in the land. Meanwhile, all that long, hot summer and into the fall, the boycott went on.

Then in November the city struck again. They took the MIA to court once more. This time they attacked the car-pool. They said it was destroying a private business— the bus line—so it should be stopped.

This new court case filled Martin with gloom. Another winter was approaching and his people were bone tired. "It's just too much to ask them to continue," he said to Coretta, "if we don't have *any* transportation at all."

The night before the judge was to hand down his decision, Martin spoke quietly to still another mass meeting. He was sure that the judge would rule against them. "So tonight we must believe that a way will be found out of no way," he said sadly.

The next day as he sat quietly in court he looked at a clock on the wall. It was almost time for lunch. "The clock said it was noon," he said later, "but it was midnight in my soul."

Just then some people began to stir and whisper at the back of the room. Moments later a reporter ran up to Martin. "Reverend," he said, "this is what you've been waiting for!" And he shoved a piece of paper into Martin's hand.

As Martin read the paper his heart began to pound. The United States Supreme

Court had just decided that all bus segregation in Alabama was unconstitutional. It was over. They had won.

That evening there was a victory celebration at the Holt Street Baptist Church. Martin Luther King had tears in his eyes as he gazed out across the big auditorium filled with people. It had been a long journey they had taken together—this one-day boycott that had grown to almost a year. And they'd won much more than the right to ride unsegregated buses.

In the beginning many had been afraid. They had been filled with what Martin called "a sense of nobodyness." But not anymore. As a black janitor put it, "We got our heads up now and we won't ever bow down again."

That was the true miracle of Montgomery.

The Movement Grows

Life would never be the same for Martin. A year ago he had been a young and unknown preacher. Now he was famous. He was known all across the United States and in other countries, too. He was Martin Luther King, Jr., leader of the fast-growing civil rights movement.

Suddenly all kinds of awards and honors began to pour in. Long articles were written about him in newspapers and magazines. He was asked to speak at meetings and dinners all across the country. He was offered many important and high-paying jobs.

One award especially pleased Martin. It was an honorary degree from Morehouse—the college he had graduated from just a few years before. He sat at the award ceremony as President Benjamin Mays said, "You are mature beyond your years. You are wiser at 28 than most men are at 60. You are more courageous than most men can ever be."

A few months later Martin and other black leaders from all across the South formed a new organization. It was called the Southern Christian Leadership Conference, the SCLC. Martin was elected its president. The SCLC had one purpose—to fight for Negro rights everywhere.

Life became a whirlwind for Martin. He helped plan other boycotts. He worked for the right to vote. He traveled hundreds of thousands of miles each year giving speeches to raise money for the SCLC. He wrote a book about the Montgomery bus boycott. And all the while he tried to be a full-time pastor at the Dexter Avenue Baptist Church.

Finally Martin realized that things could not go on this way. Sadly he told the Dexter congregation that he must leave them. He was going to become co-pastor of Ebenezer, Daddy King's church. Then he would have more time to give to the SCLC. "I can't stop now," he told his congregation. "History has thrust something on me and I cannot turn away."

Martin tells his congregation at Montgomery's Dexter Avenue Baptist Church that he must leave them.

So Martin and the family moved to Atlanta. By now that family had grown. Yoki was big sister to a little brother named for his father—but everyone called him Marty.

Just as the Kings moved into their new Home, another move was being made—a big step forward in the civil rights movement. On February 2, 1960, four Negro college students walked into a Greensboro, North Carolina, department store and sat down at the lunch counter. Negroes could buy things in the store. They could even buy food at the lunch counter—if they stood up. But only white customers could sit on one of the stools.

Nobody would serve the four black students, of course. So all day they just sat quietly. It wasn't easy. Most customers ignored what was going on. Some, however, cursed and shoved and even hit the students.

But the next day—and the next—the students were back. News of their brave action spread quickly through the colleges in the area.

*Brave college students begin a new chapter in
the civil rights struggle—the sit-in movement.*

On the fourth day some white students
from a nearby girls' school joined in the
protest. Menus were offered to these white
students. But they just shook their heads.
They would not eat until everyone was
served.

The student sit-in movement spread
like wildfire all across the South. Two

weeks later there were ten sit-ins in progress. After two months there were fifty. For the first time blacks and whites were protesting together. "It's an idea whose time has come!" Martin exclaimed proudly.

Soon it seemed that there were sit-ins everywhere. Sometimes, to end one of them, a place would be closed down. Other times the protesters were arrested.

As they marched off to jail they sang proudly:

"We are not afraid, we are not afraid,
We are not afraid today,
Oh, deep in my heart I do believe
We shall overcome some day. . . ."

"We Shall Overcome," an old hymn with new words, had become the song of the civil rights movement.

From the beginning Martin worked with the students. He begged them to follow the "Montgomery way." No matter what happened they must not hate or fight back. "Hate cannot drive out hate," he said. "Only love can do that." And this mixture of love and nonviolent action was "the weapon that cuts without wounding. It is the sword that heals."

Before long Martin decided to take part in a sit-in himself. On a crisp October morning he and a group of students sat down together at a lunch counter in Atlanta's biggest department store. A few minutes later the police arrived and arrested everyone.

When Yoki heard that her father was in jail she was very upset. She was only four, but she already knew that jails were places for bad people.

"Why, Mommy?" she asked, tears streaming down her face. "Why did Daddy go to jail?"

"I knew my children would ask this question one day," Coretta said, "and I had thought a lot about how to answer it."

Now she took Yoki on her lap and began to speak slowly. "Your daddy is a brave and kind man. He went to jail to help people. Some people don't have enough to eat. They don't have comfortable homes to live in, or enough clothes to wear. Daddy went to jail to help all people get these things."

Yoki stopped crying. But she still looked upset. "And don't worry," Coretta added softly, "your daddy will be coming back."

Coretta wondered if Yoki was old enough to understand what she'd just been told. A few days later her question was answered. Yoki had been going to a nursery school for both black and white children. Now a little white schoolmate tried to pick a fight. "Oh, *your* daddy," the little girl said in a mean tone of voice. "He's always going to jail!"

Yoki lifted her head. "Yes," she replied proudly. "He goes to jail to help people. And I'd like to go to jail with my daddy, too."

The Children's Crusade

The wall of segregation, as Martin called it, was beginning to crack a little in the early nineteen-sixties. A few lunch counters and restaurants started to serve both blacks and whites. Here and there a school or a park or a movie theater opened quietly to everyone. Every once in a while a company began to hire black workers for the first time. But in most places the wall still stood strong and high.

Martin Luther King decided it was time to meet that wall head on. "We want freedom now," he said. "We do not want freedom fed to us in teaspoons over another 150 years."

After thinking a long time, Martin decided to take his nonviolent protest to the city of Birmingham, Alabama. Almost everything was segregated in Birmingham. And its police chief, Eugene "Bull" Connor was determined to see that it stayed that way. "Let anybody just *try* to start something," he threatened, "and blood will run in the streets."

This was no empty threat. But Birmingham was where Martin knew he had to go. If the SCLC could win in Birmingham, Martin was sure they could win anywhere. "As Birmingham goes, so goes the South," he wrote.

The plan was simple. The SCLC wanted all lunch counters, washrooms, elevators, and drinking fountains in the big downtown stores to be open to everyone. And they wanted more jobs for Negroes in those stores. That was all.

Until these demands were met all Negroes would boycott the stores. They would also hold sit-ins. Most important, every day more and more people would protest by marching through the streets of Birmingham.

These marches were against city law. Many of the marchers would be arrested and thrown in jail. This was part of Martin's plan. He wanted to fill the jails. "I want this city to face itself," he said at one of the first mass meetings. "So come and

serve in our nonviolent army. Make going to jail your badge of honor."

And many of the Negro people of Birmingham did. They marched singing through the streets until they were stopped by Bull Connor and his police. "Jail 'em all!" Connor would shout. And the police would cart them away.

Martin marched with them and went to jail, too. The other protesters were

Martin leads a long line of demonstrators in Birmingham, Alabama.

placed together in large cells. But Martin was put in solitary—not even his close friend Ralph Abernathy was allowed to be with him.

Martin loved and needed people. It hurt to be so alone. For several days he was sunk in gloom. But then he pulled himself together. "I can never truly be in solitary," he told himself. "God's companionship doesn't stop at the door of a jail cell."

That afternoon a friendly guard slipped him a local newspaper. In it was a letter written by eight white ministers. It criticized Martin and everything he was trying to do.

The ministers said that he was an outsider and never should have come to Birmingham. They said that this was not the right time for such a protest. He should have waited for another, better time. They said it was dangerous.

Now, on any scraps of paper he could find, Martin began to answer their charges.

"I am in Birmingham because injustice is here," he wrote. "Nobody is an outsider in such a fight." And, "For years now I have heard the word, 'Wait!' It rings in the ears of every Negro with piercing familiarity. This 'wait' has almost always meant 'never'." And, "We are not the creators of tension. We merely bring to the surface the hidden tension that is already alive. We bring it out in the open, where it can be seen and dealt with."

Martin, shortly before he wrote "A Letter from a Birmingham Jail."

Martin wrote and wrote until he felt he had answered every one of the ministers' complaints and doubts. This 9,000-word "Letter from a Birmingham Jail" would soon become the bible of the civil rights movement.

A few days later Martin's lawyers managed to get him out of jail. But now he faced a new problem. Birmingham was a mean, tough city. Bull Connor and the other city officials were holding firm, no matter what. And little by little the people were growing tired of marching and going to jail when nothing seemed to change. "I'm afraid that this movement is faltering," Martin said. "We're in real trouble unless we can think of a different way to do this."

"Why not get college students to march?" one of his aides suggested. "Maybe even high-school kids."

That seemed like a wonderful idea. There was only one problem. The high-school and college students weren't the only ones who wanted to march. Their little brothers and sisters did, too. At first Martin ordered his aides to turn them away. "You're too young to go to jail," they were told.

But the children kept coming back— some as young as six. "We want to march with the big kids," they said. "It's our fight, too!"

Was it? This was a hard decision for Martin to make. He hated to think of children so young marching through Birmingham's dangerous streets.

But then he remembered. He remembered a time when *he* was only six and had to ask his mother, "Why can't my two best friends play with me anymore?" And he remembered how much her answer had hurt him.

Finally Martin decided to let all the children march. "I knew that they could be hurt. But I also knew that every day their minds were being hurt by segregation—and so were their spirits and souls."

So early one May morning more than a thousand children gathered at the 16th Street Baptist Church. Martin talked to them before they started out. "Be calm," he said. "And whatever happens, don't fight back." Then, singing "We Shall Overcome," they filed out of the church and into the streets.

They got only a few blocks before they came to a line of policemen. Bull Connor was standing there, too, chewing on a big, fat cigar. "Turn back," he shouted. But the children kept coming.

"Arrest 'em! Arrest 'em all!" Connor yelled. The police tried. But there were so many children that they soon ran out of police vans. They had to send for school buses to take the rest of the children to jail.

Martin saw a policeman talking to one of the marchers—a little eight-year-old girl. "What do you *want?*" he asked, as if he really wanted to know.

The little girl looked him straight in the eye. "Freedom," she answered.

This made Martin very proud. That night he told a mass meeting, "I remember an old woman in Montgomery who explained why she would continue to walk, no matter what. 'I'm doing it for my children and for my grandchildren,' she said. Now, only seven years later, the grandchildren are doing it for themselves. What we have seen in Birmingham today is a crusade—a real children's crusade!"

He was right. Nine hundred fifty-nine girls and boys were arrested that first day. But the next day 2,500 more turned up at the 16th Street Baptist Church.

"Don't get bitter," Martin told them. "Don't get tired." Now he leaned forward, smiling a little. "*Are* you tired?"

"No!" the children thundered back. Then they, too, began to march.

Bull Connor and the police were waiting for them. Some of the police had dogs, straining at their leashes. Nearby stood a group of firemen, carrying huge water hoses.

"Freedom! We want freedom!" the

children shouted. And Bull Connor answered them. But this time he didn't yell, "Lock 'em up!" This time he bellowed, "Let 'em have it!"

Suddenly policemen charged into the crowd, clubbing anyone they could reach. The firemen turned on the big hoses and powerful streams of water surged into the crowd—so powerful they knocked many to the ground. Others were smashed against the sides of buildings, their clothes almost ripped off by the force of the water.

Then the police dogs were set free. They ran wild through the children, snarling and snapping. Three marchers were badly bitten before the battle was over.

The children tried desperately to get back to the 16th Street Church. "Look at them run," Bull Connor sneered. "We sure won this one."

How wrong he was. That evening an angry Martin Luther King stood before still another mass meeting. "We are going on despite the dogs and fire hoses," he cried. "We're going on because we have started a *fire* in Birmingham that water can't put out. We're going on because we love America. And don't worry about your children who are in jail. The eyes of the world are on Birmingham!"

And they were. Millions of Americans—and more millions around the world—were shocked and disgusted by what they saw on their TV sets and read in their newspapers.

President John F. Kennedy was angry, too. "What has just happened in Birmingham makes me sick," he said. "I can well understand why Negroes are tired of being asked to be patient."

The next day more children marched and were beaten and taken to jail. By now the jails were full. And still more children volunteered to march.

Then it was Sunday, May 5th. Three thousand young people gathered at the church. They were going to march to the Birmingham jail. There they would kneel and pray—if they got there at all.

One of Birmingham's young ministers,

Reverend Charles Billups, led the march. Before long they came to the line of police and firemen. The children knelt in front of them and began to pray.

"Get up! Go back!" Bull Connor screamed. "Or you'll get everything we got!" But the children still knelt.

Now Reverend Billups stood and spoke quietly to the police and firemen. "We're not turning back. We haven't done anything wrong. All we want is our freedom. How do you feel doing these things?" Then he took a deep breath. "So bring on your dogs. Beat us up. Turn on your hoses. We're not going to retreat."

Reverend Billups started forward. Behind him came the children. "Turn on the hoses!" Bull Connor shouted. But the firemen just stood there. "Turn the dogs loose," he yelled. But the police just stood there, too. A number of these grown men

Many people in different parts of the country demonstrated in sympathy for the young civil rights marchers in Birmingham, Alabama. This group in New York City wanted to "bury" the Jim Crow laws, laws which made segregation and discrimination legal.

were openly crying as the children passed. Not a finger was raised against them.

"It was one of the most fantastic things I have ever seen," Martin Luther King said. "I was there. I felt the pride and the *power* of nonviolence." Later he added, "The last few days mark the nonviolent movement's coming of age."

The spirit of segregated Birmingham had been broken. Several days later the business leaders met with the SCLC. They agreed to every one of its demands.

The Birmingham Movement was proof indeed that soul-force was stronger than body-force. And it did what Martin hoped for most. It stirred the conscience of America.

"I Have a Dream Today . . ."

A month later President Kennedy sent a strong civil rights bill to Congress. "This nation was founded on the principle that all men are created equal," he said. "We say we are the land of the free. We *are*, except for Negroes. The time has come for America to fulfill her promise."

Martin was pleased by the President's words. But he knew that Congress had to vote for the bill before it could become law. "We need to keep the pressure up," he said.

"What about a march on Washington, D.C. itself?" someone suggested. "I really believe that as many as 100,000 people would come if you asked them to."

But would they? This was the question Martin and his fellow workers asked themselves as they started planning for this march on the nation's capital. Would they care enough to come?

Martin and Coretta arrived in Washington the day before the march. Because they would be so busy they left the children at home. There were four young Kings by now—Yoki, Marty, Dexter, and the baby girl, Bernice. Everyone called her Bunny.

All evening Martin worked on the speech he would give. The next day dawned clear and warm. At first the news was not good. "It looks as though we're only going to get about 25,000 people," an aide said.

But he was wrong. All morning—by car and bus and train and plane—people poured into Washington, D.C. Some rode bicycles. Some walked. One man even roller-skated all the way from Chicago.

On and on they came—by the thousands, by the tens of thousands. At ten o'clock there were already more than the 100,000 they had hoped for. By noon there were 200,000. And finally more than 250,000 had marched through the streets of Washington to gather on the Mall, a long, narrow park in front of the Lincoln Memorial. It was the largest march in the nation's history.

Martin sat on a platform in front of the Memorial. Around him were high government officials, other civil rights leaders, famous singers, and movie stars.

One after another they got up to speak or sing. It was a good program. But it was a long one. The day was hot, and there was almost no shade. People began to drift away. They had heard enough for one day.

Then the loudspeakers boomed out, "And now we give you—the Reverend Martin Luther King, Jr.!" At that, the crowds began to come back.

For a moment Martin just stood there.

Behind him was the great statue of Abraham Lincoln. Before him were a quarter of a million people—almost a third of them white. What a moment, he thought. What a time to be alive!

At first Martin read from the speech he had prepared so carefully. But soon he pushed it aside and began to speak the way he did best—from the heart.

"I have a dream deeply rooted in the American dream. I have a dream that one day this nation will rise up and live out the true meaning of its creed: 'We hold these truths to be self-evident, that all men are created equal.'"

The crowd had grown quiet now, as they listened eagerly to every word.

"I have a dream that my four little children will one day live in a nation where they will not be judged by the color of their skin but by the content of their character. I have a dream today. . . ."

More than 250,000 people in front of the Lincoln Memorial as Martin gives his "I Have a Dream" speech.

Martin went on, sharing his dream of a time when "all God's children, black men and white men, Jews and Gentiles, Protestants and Catholics, will be able to join hands and sing in the words of that old Negro spiritual, 'Free at last! Free at last! Thank God almighty, we are free at last!'"

There was a hush after Martin reached the end of his speech. Then the huge crowd began to clap and cheer for Martin's dream of a new America. Many were crying. And two women who had been strangers before—one white and one black—turned and hugged each other.

For Martin it was a year of triumphs—that year of 1963. First there had been the victory in Birmingham. Then the March on Washington. And *Time* magazine picked him as their "Man of the Year."

But it was a year of tragedies, too. A beloved civil rights leader, Medgar Evers, was shot. Only three weeks after the March on Washington, a bomb exploded in a Birmingham Sunday school class. Four little girls were killed.

Then came the worst tragedy of all. It was November 22, 1963. Martin was in the upstairs bedroom, packing to go off on a trip. The television was on in the background. Suddenly an emergency news bulletin interrupted the program. For a few stunned seconds Martin just stared at the screen. Then "Corrie!" he shouted. "President Kennedy has been shot by someone—maybe killed!"

Coretta rushed into the bedroom. She and Martin sat side by side on the bed, listening to the awful news that the President was dead. Finally Martin said very quietly, "This is going to happen to me, too."

Oh, no, Coretta wanted to say. But she couldn't. She couldn't find a single word of comfort—because she was afraid he might be right. Just as millions of people loved Martin Luther King, so some hated everything he stood for. All Coretta could do was move closer and grip his hand in hers.

Martin enjoys a rare moment at home.

The Greatest Award of All

Martin's work often took him away from home for days or weeks at a time. Whenever he returned he would open the front door very quietly and call out, "Where is everyone?" Then Coretta and the children would come rushing to greet him.

Oh, how the children loved these times when their daddy was home. Martin could seem very serious when he was giving a speech or leading a march. But at home he was full of fun—teasing and tickling and roughhousing with Yoki and Marty and Dexter and Bunny.

One of his favorite things to do was to have one of the children stand halfway up the stairs leading to the second floor. He'd open his arms wide and the child would leap off into space—only to be caught at the last moment.

"He was like a child himself," Coretta remembered. "Sometimes things got so wild that I thought they were going to take the house apart."

But she just smiled and went out to the kitchen to start fixing some of Martin's favorite dishes. What he liked best were what he called "real down-home foods" like pork chops, fried chicken, pigs' feet, black-eyed peas, and turnip greens. "There's no doubt about it," Martin would often chuckle, "eating is one of my *major* sins."

But all too soon it would be time for Martin to pack his suitcase once more. This made the children sad, of course. It also made them proud. "Daddy's away helping other people," Coretta had taught them. "When he's finished, he'll be back."

"That's right," young Marty would add. "Daddy's out fixing things."

Martin Luther King had been given hundreds of awards and medals and honorary degrees. One day in October of 1964 the phone rang at the King house. Coretta picked it up to hear a reporter ask, "Have you heard the news?"

"What news?" she answered.

"Your husband has just won the Nobel Peace Prize for 1964." An international committee had decided that he was the person who had done the most for peace that year in the world.

Martin and Coretta flew to Oslo, Norway, to accept the prize. He sat on the stage of a big auditorium. Before him in the audience sat the King of Norway and many other important people. Slowly the king rose to his feet. Then he began to clap. Soon everyone was standing, clapping the Baptist preacher from the United States of America.

Then Dr. Gunnar Jahn, chairman of the Nobel Committee, introduced Martin as "the first person in the western world to have shown us that a struggle can be waged without violence."

Trumpets blared. Martin stepped forward to accept his award. He didn't accept it for himself, he said. He accepted it for the millions of Negroes in the United States who were part of the battle to end "the long night of racial injustice."

Most of these people would never make the headlines, he continued, but one day "we will have a finer land, a better people, a more noble civilization—because these humble children of God were willing to suffer."

After the awards ceremony Martin and Coretta visited different places in Europe. Everywhere they went they were cheered by crowds of people. Many American cities honored Martin, too. But what pleased him most was a big dinner given for him by 1,500 black and white citizens of his hometown of Atlanta.

*Martin and Coretta hug after he received the
Nobel Peace Prize. Martin was just 35 years old
—the youngest man ever to receive the prize.*

Martin's eyes sparkled with excitement
as he looked out across the room that
night. He was remembering a little boy
who wasn't allowed to sit in the front of a
shoe store in this very town. He was remembering a man who only five years ago
had been arrested for sitting at a nearby
lunch counter. Yet here blacks and whites
were eating and talking happily—
together.

"Bloody Sunday"

After dinner Martin rose to say a few words. "These past few weeks I have been on a mountaintop," he said. "And I really wish I could just stay on that mountain. But I must go back to the valley. I must go back because there are people who can't vote in the valley, and people who are starving, and people who don't have jobs. . . . "

For Martin Luther King the next valley was a place called Selma, Alabama. He and the SCLC staff had decided to hold a voting rights drive there. Half the people in Selma were black. But only one out of a hundred of them could vote. Officials used any excuse to keep them from registering—hard tests, tricks, threats, anything. One man was even rejected because he forgot to cross a "t" on his registration form.

Martin was determined to change all this. At the first mass meeting held at Browns Chapel Church, he said, "Our cry is a simple one. Give us the ballot! We're not on our knees begging for the ballot. We are demanding the ballot!"

The next day he led the first group to the county courthouse. But there was a law in Selma that no more than 20 people could march together at a time. And the city was determined to enforce this law. "I've been keeping blacks in their place for years," Sheriff Jim Clark bragged, "and I don't aim to stop now."

So most of the marchers were arrested and thrown in jail. But the next day more people took their place. After a few weeks the protest began to spread to nearby towns. Then tragedy struck. On one of these peaceful marches a teenage boy named Jimmie Lee Jackson was shot and killed.

When Martin heard about Jimmie Lee's death he called for another march—a march from Selma all the way to the State Capitol in Montgomery, to protest this senseless murder.

"I can't promise you that it won't get your house bombed," Martin told his people. "I can't promise you that it won't get you beaten up. But we must stand up for what is right!"

Governor George Wallace didn't agree. He issued an order to stop the march. And he told his state police to see that the order was enforced "any way you have to."

Martin was not in Selma on the day of the march. He was in Atlanta taking care of some important SCLC business. Early that Sunday morning more than 500 people gathered in front of Browns Chapel Church to start the 50-mile trip.

They walked through the streets of Selma until they came to the Edmund Pettus Bridge on the edge of town. On the far side of the bridge stood a group of state troopers, blocking the highway.

"Halt!" one of the troopers called out, as the others put on gas masks. "You have two minutes to turn around and go back to your church."

The seconds ticked by—and nobody moved. Then came the order, "Troopers, advance!"

Some of the troopers hurled tear gas. Others charged, swinging nightsticks. Still others rode on horseback through the helpless crowd, slashing at them with heavy whips.

The marchers had no choice. They were forced back to the safety of the Browns Chapel Church. But seventy of them didn't make it—they were in the hospital instead. Soon people began to call that day "Bloody Sunday."

When Martin heard what had happened he raced back to Selma. He called for a second march to Montgomery. But this time, he said, it was not to be just a local march. He sent out a call for religious leaders from across the nation to join them in Selma. "The black people of Selma will struggle on for the soul of America," he said. "But it is fitting that all Americans help to bear the burden."

And many Americans were willing. Before the week was out more than 400 ministers, nuns, priests, and rabbis—almost all of them white—had arrived in Selma. They were all eager to join the march for justice.

But before this march could take place, tragedy struck once more. Three white ministers had eaten dinner in one of Selma's black restaurants. As they were leaving, they were attacked. The Reverend

James Reeb of Boston was struck on the head with a club. Two days later he was dead.

This death shocked the whole nation. In cities and towns across the land blacks and whites marched to protest the bloody events taking place in Selma. And President Lyndon Johnson voiced what many were now feeling.

"The real hero of this struggle is the American Negro. His actions and protests, his courage to risk safety, and even to risk his life, have awakened the conscience of this nation."

A few days later more than 3,000 people gathered at Browns Chapel Church. The Selma-to-Montgomery March was about to begin once more.

Martin marched in the front row as they set out. Some of the others in that first row were a rabbi, a priest, a nun, and a representative of the United Nations.

Singing "We Shall Overcome," they crossed the Edmund Pettus Bridge and headed down Highway 80 toward Montgomery. On either side of the highway were members of the Alabama National Guard and the United States Army—ordered by the President to protect the marchers.

They marched seven miles that day before they set up camp for the night. As Martin drifted off to sleep in his tent, he listened to a group of young people, black and white, from all across America. They were singing, "Many good men have lived and died, so we could be marching side by side. . . ."

Late the next day they came to a dusty little Negro town called Trickem Crossroads. Standing in front of a tumbledown school were some grown-ups and a few children. Martin walked over to talk with them. An old woman reached up and kissed him. "God will keep His arms around you," she whispered.

"Yes," Martin said. "And you, too."

As they left town an old man hobbled

along beside them. "I just want to walk a little ways with you," he said. "I figure I been called 'boy' long enough."

On the morning of the fifth day the journey ended. With Coretta by his side, Martin led 25,000 people through the familiar streets of Montgomery to the State Capitol.

Here's where it all started, he thought. *So much has happened in the ten years since the bus boycott. Since the day Rosa Parks decided not to get up. We've come such a long way. . . .*

Standing on the steps of the Capitol, Martin looked out across the people before him. Many of them had just finished a march of 50 miles. Fifty miles didn't sound like much—unless you knew that it stood for years of struggle and danger and suffering.

Now Martin began to speak. "They told us we wouldn't get here," he said. "And there were those who said that we would get here only over their dead bodies. But

all the world today knows that we are here, and standing before the forces of power in the State of Alabama saying, 'We ain't goin' let *nobody* turn us around.' So I stand before you today with the conviction that segregation is on its death bed.''

Martin, with Coretta by his side, leads 25,000 people through the streets at the end of the five-day Selma-to-Montgomery march.

As usual after one of Martin's speeches everyone joined hands to sing "We Shall Overcome." Except that now they changed one word. Today they sang "We *Have* Overcome."

The Poor People's March

Because of what happened in Selma, President Johnson asked Congress to pass a bill that would truly protect the Negro's right to vote. And before the summer was over they did. This bill became the Voting Rights Act of 1965.

"Today is a triumph for freedom as great as any victory that's ever been won on any battlefield," President Johnson said as he signed the bill into law.

He was right. A great battle had been won. But the war was far from over. For

Every year Martin traveled hundreds of thousands of miles. "Sometimes I get so tired," he told friends, "but I can't stop."

10 years Martin had been working to end segregation. Now, in the mid-1960's, he began to think more and more about poverty. Segregation was mainly a Southern problem. But poverty crippled the lives of black people all across America.

"What good does it do to be able to sit at a lunch counter, if you don't have the money to pay for a hamburger?" he asked.

It was true. In cities across the land blacks lived in terrible slums. Their homes were tumbledown. Many could not find work. Many went hungry. Yet they knew that there *was* a better life—for other people. And this was making them more and more angry.

One hot August night in 1965 that anger exploded. It became a bloody riot in a place called Watts—a black neighborhood in Los Angeles.

It began when a white policeman tried to arrest a black man. A crowd began to gather. The man fought back a little. The policeman was a little too rough. Someone threw a bottle at him. Someone else set fire to a nearby car. And the riot was on.

It raged for days. Before it was over 34 people were dead. Almost a thousand were badly hurt. Millions of dollars worth of property—homes and cars and stores—had been destroyed. It was one of the worst race riots in American history.

Martin flew out to Watts. He walked

the streets and tried to calm people. He tried to make them understand that rioting was not the answer to their problems. "Violence only leads to violence," he said again and again. "Hate cannot drive out hate. Only love can do that."

But most people would not listen. "Burn, baby, burn!" they shouted. And one teenager announced, "We won!"

Martin was stunned. "How can you say you *won*, when 34 Negroes are dead? How can you say you won, when your community is destroyed?"

"We won," the youngster answered, "because we made people pay attention to us."

A number of black leaders agreed. "If America doesn't come around, we're going to burn America down," one announced. Another said, "I'm not for that nonviolent stuff anymore. The time for peaceful marches is over."

Martin spoke out against this sort of thinking with all his strength. "If every

Negro in the United States turns to violence, I will be the one lone voice preaching that this is the wrong way," he said. "We must continue to work for first-class citizenship, but we must never use second-class methods to gain it."

But sometimes he got so worn out. How nice it would be to stop struggling, to stop fighting for what he knew was right. "I don't mind saying, I'm tired of marching," he admitted. "I'm tired of marching for something that should have been mine at birth. I don't mind saying to you, I'm tired of living every day under the threat of death. I want to live as long as anybody. And sometimes I begin to doubt whether I'm going to make it. So I'll tell anybody, I'm willing to stop marching. I don't march because I like it. I march because I must."

Martin knew how dangerous his work was. He began to talk more and more about dying. "If anything happens to me, you must be prepared to continue," he told his SCLC staff.

One day he sent Coretta some flowers. They were beautiful red carnations. But when she touched them she realized they were not real. It was strange—Martin had never done anything like this before.

When he came home she kissed him and thanked him for the flowers. "They're beautiful, and they're plastic," she said.

"Yes," Martin answered, "I wanted to give you something you could always keep." Those were the last flowers she ever got from him.

But Martin didn't let the threat of death stop him. Early in 1968 he began to plan for the biggest march of all—a poor people's march on Washington, D.C.

"We're going to reach out to poor people all across the United States," he said. "We're going to ask American Indians to come to Washington and stay there until something is done to make their lives better. We're going to ask Spanish-Americans to come . . . and poor whites . . . for poverty isn't just a black problem. It's a *human* problem that must be solved."

"Black and White Together, We Shall Overcome. . . ."

The Poor People's March was planned for April. But a month before then, Martin was asked to go to Memphis, Tennessee. Black garbage workers there were striking for higher pay. The city government was not paying any attention to their demands. So the strike leaders wanted Martin to come to their city and lead a march. Maybe then they could get some action.

Martin didn't want to go. He was far too busy. "But these are poor folks," he told his staff. "What is the point of going

The governor of Tennessee called out the National Guard when black garbage workers were asking for equal pay and equal treatment.

to Washington in April if we don't stop for them?"

On the day of the march in Memphis, Martin took his place in the front row. But the march had barely begun when he heard a crash, and the sound of shattering glass. Some teenagers were smashing store windows. Now the police had an excuse to move in.

"Call it off," Martin cried. "I will never lead a violent march!"

Martin was very sad as he flew back to Atlanta. Nothing like this had ever happened before. "I'll have to go back and lead a second march," he told his aides, "for nonviolence itself is on trial in Memphis."

A week later Martin and his co-workers returned. For the next few days they would work with the people of Memphis to see that *this* march stayed peaceful.

That first evening Martin spoke at a mass rally. He spoke about what a wonderful life he'd had. He talked about how happy he was to be alive in these times— no matter what troubles and problems the times brought. "So it really doesn't matter what happens with me now," he said. "Because I have been to the mountaintop. And I've looked over, and I've seen the promised land. I may not get there with you. But I want you to know tonight that we as a people will get to the promised land. So

I'm happy tonight. I'm not worried about anything. I'm not fearing any man. Mine eyes have seen the glory of the coming of the Lord!"

It was Martin Luther King's last speech.

The next day he spent quietly in his room at the Lorraine Motel, working on plans for the Poor People's March. Just before suppertime he stepped onto the balcony for a breath of fresh air.

"Hey, Doc!" one of his aides called from the parking lot below. "You better put a coat on. It's getting chilly."

"Okay," Martin said with a grin, "I'll do it." He started to turn toward his room. Then there was the sound of a single shot. And Martin slumped to the floor of the balcony.

He had said it so often. "I'm not going to live a long life." He was right. Martin Luther King, Jr., was dead at 39. His killer was James Earl Ray—a white man who hated him and all other blacks.

All across America—all across the

world—people felt a deep sense of loss. Some tried to put their feelings about what had happened into words.

Jacqueline Kennedy, the widow of President John F. Kennedy, wrote a letter to Coretta. She asked, "When will our country learn that to live by the sword is to perish by the sword?"

Other people tried to express what Martin had meant to them. "It isn't how long one lives, but how well," said Dr. Benjamin Mays, the President of Morehouse College.

"The grave is too narrow for his soul," a friend in the civil rights movement mourned.

"He had a way of giving people the feeling that they could be bigger and stronger, more courageous and loving than they thought they could be," someone else added.

Coretta and the children. This photo was taken after Martin's death, on the airplane that brought his body back to Atlanta.

President Johnson ordered that the American flag fly at half-staff until after Martin's funeral. And from all across the country people began to stream into Atlanta. They wanted to say a final good-bye to the gentle dreamer.

On the day of the funeral thousands gathered at Ebenezer Baptist Church. There they listened as his deep voice rolled out one last time—for someone had recorded a sermon he had given a few months before.

In that sermon Martin said he didn't want to be remembered because he'd won a Nobel Peace Prize. That wasn't important. "I'd like someone to mention that day that Martin Luther King, Jr., tried to give his life serving others. I'd like for somebody to say that Martin Luther King, Jr., tried to love somebody."

After the funeral service Martin's coffin was placed on an old farm wagon—a wagon Martin had planned to use during the Poor People's March. Two Georgia mules pulled it through the streets of Atlanta. Behind it almost 100,000 people walked—rich and poor, famous and unknown, black and white. It was Martin Luther King's last march.

At the cemetery there was another brief service. Then everyone joined hands and sang, "Black and white together, we shall overcome one day...."

Martin would have liked that.